Documents from the National Archives

Watergate

Produced by the Education Branch, Office of Public Programs

National Archives and Records Administration
in cooperation with

American Historical Association

Community College Humanities Association

Organization of American Historians

Board of Consultants:

American Historical Association:
Jane Turner Censer, George Mason University
Gerald A. Danzer, University of Illinois at Chicago

Community College Humanities Association:
Joan M. Crouse, Hilbert College
Karen Olson, Dundalk Community College

Organization of American Historians:
Joseph C. Morton, Northeastern University
John T. Schlotterbeck, DePauw University

KENDALL/HUNT PUBLISHING COMPANY
2460 Kerper Boulevard P.O. Box 539 Dubuque, Iowa 52004-0539

Other Learning Packages in this series include:

Documents from the National Archives: Internment of Japanese Americans

Documents from the National Archives: Women in Industry—World War II

ISBN 0-8403-7401-1

Printed in the United States of America
10 9 8 7 6 5 4 3 2 1

Documents from the National Archives:
Watergate

House Calendar No. 426

93D CONGRESS } HOUSE OF REPRESENTATIVES { REPORT
2d Session } { No. 93–1305

IMPEACHMENT OF RICHARD M. NIXON, PRESIDENT OF
THE UNITED STATES

AUGUST 20, 1974—Referred to the House Calendar and ordered to be printed

Mr. RODINO, from the Committee on the Judiciary,
submitted the following

REPORT

Contents

Foreword

To make the historical records of the federal government available nationally, the National Archives has begun a program to introduce these vast resources to college-level students and other adult learners, expanding a program begun in 1979 for secondary school students and teachers.

Documents from the National Archives: Watergate is the first learning package in this series. For their assistance, we are grateful to the American Historical Association, the Commu-

> ECT: Factors to be Considered in Deciding Whether t
>   Prosecute Richard M. Nixon for Obstruction of
>   Justice
>
>   In our view there is clear evidence that Richard
> ticipated in a conspiracy to obstruct justice by co
>   identity of those responsible for the Watergate br
> other criminal offenses. There is a presumption (

nity College Humanities Association, and the Organization of American Historians and to the consultants from those associations who advised us. We are sure that students' understanding of Watergate will be expanded by using these documents. But we also hope that they will feel the excitement and widened curiosity that comes from reading a document created by someone who participated in or witnessed a major historical event. This experience is a significant one, shared by archivists and historians alike.

DON W. WILSON
Archivist of the United States

●Preface

About this Series

The National Archives and Records Administration preserves and makes available the historically valuable records created by the federal government and encourages the use of these resources. Toward that end, the

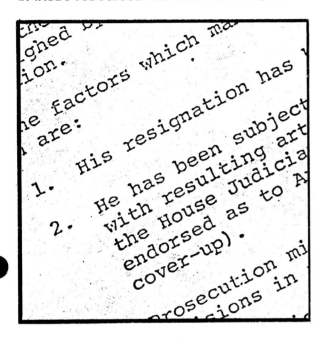

Archives has provided this series of reproduced documents on several topics for use in college classrooms or with other adult audiences.

Using archival records can be fascinating because the documents are authentic, personal, and touched by the lives of people from the past. Correctly read, they can reveal facts, points of view, bias, and contradictions. The evidence they offer requires careful scrutiny and often lends itself to more than one interpretation. By analyzing documents, we understand more clearly that secondary sources are derivative.

We have selected the documents in this package from among hundreds that the Archives holds on this topic. These few do not begin to tell the whole story of Watergate, but they do suggest some of the issues involved. They also offer an opportunity for the reader to use raw materials and to practice interpreting them.

Acknowledgments

No publication of this kind can be done entirely by the people whose names appear below. We thank all those archivists, educators, and critics who helped us to produce this unit. In particular, without the informed and generous help of David Paynter, Rod Ross, Steve Tilley, and Milton Gustafson, the search for and reproduction of records in the National Archives would have been far more difficult.

Our Board of Consultants, whose names are listed on the title page, responded promptly and completely to our request for criticism of the draft package, and their comments have shaped and improved it. James Gardner, American Historical Association; David Berry, Community College Humanities Association; and Arnita Jones, Organization of American Historians, were immensely helpful in providing suggestions for the makeup of this board. Linda N. Brown, Assistant Archivist for Public Programs, and Edith James, Director of the Exhibits and Educational Programs Division, reviewed the text. The manuscript was ably edited by Sandra M. Tilley.

Linda Henry and *Jean West*
Education Specialists
National Archives and Records Administration

Elsie T. Freeman, Chief
Education Branch
National Archives and Records Administration

•Introduction

A Historical Context for these Documents

In August 1974 Richard M. Nixon became the first American President ever to resign his office, a direct result of events known as "Watergate." The episode began June 17, 1972, when five burglars were arrested at the Democratic National Committee Headquarters in the Watergate office building in Washington, DC. The burglars had in their possession documents linking them with the Committee to Re-Elect the President. Nevertheless, the Nixon administration dismissed the episode as a "third-rate burglary," and Nixon was reelected by a landslide in November. Suspicions about Watergate persisted, however, and ultimately all branches of government became involved in investigations and decisions.

News reporters, particularly Bob Woodward and Carl Bernstein of the *Washington Post,* and congressional committees continued to uncover information about clandestine and criminal activities that pointed to White House involvement. In January 1973 four of the burglars and E. Howard Hunt pleaded guilty to the break-in, and G. Gordon Liddy and James McCord were convicted of burglary. The investigation broadened when a federal district court grand jury, with Judge John Sirica presiding, and the Senate Select Committee on Presidential Campaign Activities, chaired by Sam Ervin, began to investigate the break-in and related activities.

In April, as Watergate revelations pointed not only to White House involvement but also to a White House coverup, H. R. Haldeman and John D. Ehrlichman, Nixon's closest aides, and Attorney General Richard Kleindienst resigned. At the same time, the President fired his White House Counsel, John W. Dean.

In May Archibald Cox was appointed to head the Office of the Watergate Special Prosecutor in the Justice Department and was charged with continuing the investigations begun by the U.S. Attorney. The Senate Select Committee also began its televised hearings, during which Dean testified that the White House had been involved in a coverup of high-level involvement in Watergate and other illegal activities. Furthermore, a Haldeman aide revealed the startling information that for years Nixon had secretly tape-recorded most Presidential conversations and telephone calls in the Oval Office and in his office in the Old Executive Office Building. The committee and the Prosecutor promptly subpoenaed the tapes, but Nixon refused to comply, citing executive privilege and national security.

The struggle for access to the tapes was fought in the courts throughout the summer of 1973, with both the U.S. district court and the court of appeals ruling that the President had to turn over the tapes to the Special Prosecutor. The President offered to supply verified tape transcripts, but Special Prosecutor Cox could not accept this compromise. In October Nixon fired Cox and returned the investigation to the Department of Justice. The subsequent public out-cry against the so-called "Saturday Night Massacre," along with pressure from the Congress, forced Nixon to appoint a new Special Prosecutor, Leon Jaworski.

By the beginning of 1974, the House Committee on the Judiciary began deliberations regarding impeachment. In March the grand jury indicted Haldeman, Ehrlichman, former Attorney General John Mitchell, and others for prejury and obstruction of justice, named Nixon an "unindicted co-conspirator," and forwarded the evidence to the House Judiciary Committee.

Struggles for access to additional tapes continued. In April Nixon released edited transcripts to the House Judiciary Committee for use in its investigation, but he refused to provide copies of any additional tape recordings. In July, however, a unanimous Supreme Court forced Nixon to surrender the actual tape recordings. A week later, upon hearing the evidence within, the House Judiciary Committee adopted three articles of impeachment against the President, charging him with obstruction of justice, misuse of powers, and refusal to obey House subpoenas. President Nixon resigned the Presidency on August 9, 1974. President Gerald R. Ford pardoned Nixon

H   Now, on the investigation, you know the Democratic

break-in thing, we're back in the problem area because

the FBI is not under control, because Gray doesn't exa

know how to control it and they have - their investigatio

is now leading into some productive areas - because th

on September 8, 1974.

The documents in this package concern three questions that Americans and their government grappled with during the Watergate episode: Should President Nixon have been impeached, should he have been prosecuted, and should he have been pardoned? This package contains only a few documents for each question, but they provide a sampling of Watergate records. They also suggest why Americans held differing interpretations about Watergate at the time, as they do today.

The documents are from several record groups held by the National Archives and Records Administration. Document #3 contains two excerpts from transcripts of the tapes as used by the House Judiciary Committee, the full text of which comprises several hundred pages. "Unintelligible" appears frequently in the transcripts because sound quality was poor, other noises obscured conversations, and begining words and low conversations were usually lost. The back cover shows a diagram of the Oval Office with the placement of microphones, labeled M-1, M-2, etc. The tapes themselves are surely among the most famous of primary sources. Researchers can listen to unexpurgated copies of them, as played for the jury in *U.S. v. Mitchell et al.*, at the National Archives in Washington, DC.

Cast of Characters

Charles W. Colson	Special Counsel to the President
Kenneth H. Dahlberg	Fundraiser for the Nixon reelection campaign
John W. Dean III	Counsel to the President
John D. Ehrlichman	Assistant to the President for Domestic Affairs
Carl B. Feldbaum	Staff member, Watergate Special Prosecutor's Office
Gerald R. Ford	President of the United States succeeding Richard M. Nixon
L. Patrick Gray III	Acting Director, Federal Bureau of Investigation
Alexander M. Haig, Jr.	White House Chief of Staff succeeding Haldeman
H. R. "Bob" Haldeman	White House Chief of Staff
Richard M. Helms	Director, Central Intelligence Agency
E. Howard Hunt	Former CIA agent and member of the White House "Plumbers" unit
Leon Jaworski	Watergate Special Prosecutor
Henry A. Kissinger	Secretary of State succeeding William P. Rogers
Peter M. Kreindler	Staff member, Watergate Special Prosecutor's Office
Philip A. Lacovara	Counsel to the Watergate Special Prosecutor
G. Gordon Liddy	Former FBI agent and member of the White House "Plumbers" unit
John N. Mitchell	Attorney General of the United States
Richard M. Nixon	President of the United States
William P. Rogers	Secretary of State
James D. St. Clair	Special Counsel to the President
Maurice H. Stans	Secretary of Commerce
Vernon A. Walters	Deputy Director, Central Intelligence Agency
Rose Mary Woods	Personal Secretary to the President

Introduction to Document Analysis

As you read the documents that follow, consider the following questions. They will sharpen your understanding of the document and your critical skills. You will find it helpful to write down your responses to these questions.

1. What type of document are you reading?

Newspaper	Map	Report
Letter	Telegram	Legal decision
Press release	Deposition	Photograph
Memorandum	Pamphlet	Other
Cartoon	Advertisement	

2. What are the unique physical characteristics of this document?

Letterhead	Notations	Handwriting
Typeface	Typing	Seals
Stamps: "Received" or other	Illustrations	Other

3. What is the date of the document?

4. Who is the author or creator of the document?

5. For what audience or for whom was the document created?

6. What information does this document provide about the following? (There are many possible ways to answer these questions.)

   a. What has the author of this document said that you think is important? List three points.

   b. Why do you think the document was created?

   c. What evidence in the document helps you to know why it was written?

   d. What does the document tell you about life in the United States at the time it was created?

7. Ask the document's creator a question that is left unanswered by the document.

List of Documents

Records in the National Archives are filed by Record Group (RG).

1. Cover: Richard M. Nixon's letter of resignation, August 9, 1974. Letters of Resignation and Declination of Federal Office, General Records of the Department of State, RG 59.

2. House of Representatives Committee on the Judiciary Report on Impeachment of Richard M. Nixon, August 20, 1974. Records of the U.S. House of Representatives, RG 233.

3. Transcript excerpts (pp. 39–46, 54–55), June 23, 1972. Hearings Before the Committee on the Judiciary, House of Representatives, Publications of the U.S. Government, RG 287.

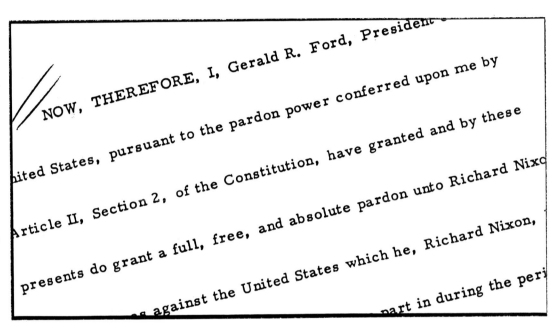

4. Memorandum by Vernon Walters, June 28, 1972. Hearings Before the Committee on the Judiciary, House of Representatives, Publications of the U.S. Government, RG 287.

5. Memorandum from Carl B. Feldbaum and Peter M. Kreindler to Leon Jaworski about factors to consider in prosecuting Nixon, August 9, 1974. Records of the Watergate Special Prosecution Force, RG 460.

6. *Washington Post* article about Watergate public opinion, August 26, 1974. Records of the Watergate Special Prosecution Force, RG 460.

7. Memorandum from Philip A. Lacovara to Leon Jaworski about pardoning Nixon, September 5, 1974. Records of the Watergate Special Prosecution Force, RG 460.

8. President Ford's draft remarks on granting a pardon to Nixon, September 8, 1974, Gerald R. Ford Library.

9. Back cover: Diagram of Oval Office showing location of microphones, Misc. 47–73, Records of District Courts of the United States, RG 21.

THE WHITE HOUSE

WASHINGTON

August 9, 1974

Dear Mr. Secretary:

I hereby resign the Office of President of the
United States.

Sincerely,

Richard Nixon

11.35 AM

HK

The Honorable Henry A. Kissinger
The Secretary of State
Washington, D.C. 20520

House Calendar No. 426

93D CONGRESS } HOUSE OF REPRESENTATIVES { REPORT
2d Session }   { No. 93–1305

IMPEACHMENT OF RICHARD M. NIXON, PRESIDENT OF THE UNITED STATES

———

AUGUST 20, 1974—Referred to the House Calendar and ordered to be printed

———

Mr. RODINO, from the Committee on the Judiciary,
submitted the following

REPORT

together with

SUPPLEMENTAL, ADDITIONAL, SEPARATE, DISSENTING, MINORITY, INDIVIDUAL AND CONCURRING VIEWS

The Committee on the Judiciary, to whom was referred the consideration of recommendations concerning the exercise of the constitutional power to impeach Richard M. Nixon, President of the United States, having considered the same, reports thereon pursuant to H. Res. 803 as follows and recommends that the House exercise its constitutional power to impeach Richard M. Nixon, President of the United States, and that articles of impeachment be exhibited to the Senate as follows:

RESOLUTION

Impeaching Richard M. Nixon, President of the United States, of high crimes and misdemeanors.

Resolved, That Richard M. Nixon, President of the United States, is impeached for high crimes and misdemeanors, and that the following articles of impeachment be exhibited to the Senate:

Articles of impeachment exhibited by the House of Representatives of the United States of America in the name of itself and of all of the people of the United States of America, against Richard M. Nixon, President of the United States of America, in maintenance and support of its impeachment against him for high crimes and misdemeanors.

ARTICLE I

In his conduct of the office of President of the United States, Richard M. Nixon, in violation of his constitutional oath faithfully

(1)

to execute the office of President of the United States and, to the best of his ability, preserve, protect, and defend the Constitution of the United States, and in violation of his constitutional duty to take care that the laws be faithfully executed, has prevented, obstructed, and impeded the administration of justice, in that:

On June 17, 1972, and prior thereto, agents of the Committee for the Re-election of the President committed unlawful entry of the headquarters of the Democratic National Committee in Washington, District of Columbia, for the purpose of securing political intelligence. Subsequent thereto, Richard M. Nixon, using the powers of his high office, engaged personally and through his subordinates and agents, in a course of conduct or plan designed to delay, impede, and obstruct the investigation of such unlawful entry; to cover up, conceal and protect those responsible; and to conceal the existence and scope of other unlawful covert activities.

The means used to implement this course of conduct or plan included one or more of the following:

(1) making or causing to be made false or misleading statements to lawfully authorized investigative officers and employees of the United States;

(2) withholding relevant and material evidence or information from lawfully authorized investigative officers and employees of the United States;

(3) approving, condoning, acquiescing in, and counseling witnesses with respect to the giving of false or misleading statements to lawfully authorized investigative officers and employees of the United States and false or misleading testimony in duly instituted judicial and congressional proceedings;

(4) interfering or endeavoring to interfere with the conduct of investigations by the Department of Justice of the United States, the Federal Bureau of Investigation, the Office of Watergate Special Prosecution Force, and Congressional Committees;

(5) approving, condoning, and acquiescing in, the surreptitious payment of substantial sums of money for the purpose of obtaining the silence or influencing the testimony of witnesses, potential witnesses or individuals who participated in such unlawful entry and other illegal activities;

(6) endeavoring to misuse the Central Intelligence Agency, an agency of the United States;

(7) disseminating information received from officers of the Department of Justice of the United States to subjects of investigations conducted by lawfully authorized investigative officers and employees of the United States, for the purpose of aiding and assisting such subjects in their attempts to avoid criminal liability;

(8) making false or misleading public statements for the purpose of deceiving the people of the United States into believing that a thorough and complete investigation had been conducted with respect to allegations of misconduct on the part of personnel of the executive branch of the United States and personnel of the Committee for the Re-election of the President, and that there was no involvement of such personnel in such misconduct; or

(9) endeavoring to cause prospective defendants, and individuals duly tried and convicted, to expect favored treatment and

consideration in return for their silence or false testimony, or rewarding individuals for their silence or false testimony.

In all of this, Richard M. Nixon has acted in a manner contrary to his trust as President and subversive of constitutional government, to the great prejudice of the cause of law and justice and to the manifest injury of the people of the United States.

Wherefore Richard M. Nixon, by such conduct, warrants impeachment and trial, and removal from office.

Article II

Using the powers of the office of President of the United States, Richard M. Nixon, in violation of his constitutional oath faithfully to execute the office of President of the United States and, to the best of his ability, preserve, protect, and defend the Constitution of the United States, and in disregard of his constitutional duty to take care that the laws be faithfully executed, has repeatedly engaged in conduct violating the constitutional rights of citizens, impairing the due and proper administration of justice and the conduct of lawful inquiries, or contravening the laws governing agencies of the executive branch and the purposes of these agencies.

This conduct has included one or more of the following:

(1) He has, acting personally and through his subordinates and agents, endeavored to obtain from the Internal Revenue Service, in violation of the constitutional rights of citizens, confidential information contained in income tax returns for purposes not authorized by law, and to cause, in violation of the constitutional rights of citizens, income tax audits or other income tax investigations to be initiated or conducted in a discriminatory manner.

(2) He misused the Federal Bureau of Investigation, the Secret Service, and other executive personnel, in violation or disregard of the constitutional rights of citizens, by directing or authorizing such agencies or personnel to conduct or continue electronic surveillance or other investigations for purposes unrelated to national security, the enforcement of laws, or any other lawful function of his office; he did direct, authorize, or permit the use of information obtained thereby for purposes unrelated to national security, the enforcement of laws, or any other lawful function of his office; and he did direct the concealment of certain records made by the Federal Bureau of Investigation of electronic surveillance.

(3) He has, acting personally and through his subordinates and agents, in violation or disregard of the constitutional rights of citizens, authorized and permitted to be maintained a secret investigative unit within the office of the President, financed in part with money derived from campaign contributions, which unlawfully utilized the resources of the Central Intelligence Agency, engaged in covert and unlawful activities, and attempted to prejudice the constitutional right of an accused to a fair trial.

(4) He has failed to take care that the laws were faithfully executed by failing to act when he knew or had reason to know that his close subordinates endeavored to impede and frustrate

lawful inquiries by duly constituted executive, judicial, and legislative entities concerning the unlawful entry into the headquarters of the Democratic National Committee, and the cover-up thereof, and concerning other unlawful activities, including those relating to the confirmation of Richard Kleindienst as Attorney General of the United States, the electronic surveillance of private citizens, the break-in into the offices of Dr. Lewis Fielding, and the campaign financing practices of the Committee to Re-elect the President.

(5) In disregard of the rule of law, he knowingly misused the executive power by interfering with agencies of the executive branch, including the Federal Bureau of Investigation, the Criminal Division, and the Office of Watergate Special Prosecution Force, of the Department of Justice, and the Central Intelligence Agency, in violation of his duty to take care that the laws be faithfully executed.

In all of this, Richard M. Nixon has acted in a manner contrary to his trust as President and subversive of constitutional government, to the great prejudice of the cause of law and justice and to the manifest injury of the people of the United States.

Wherefore Richard M. Nixon, by such conduct, warrants impeachment and trial, and removal from office.

ARTICLE III

In his conduct of the office of President of the United States, Richard M. Nixon, contrary to his oath faithfully to execute the office of President of the United States and, to the best of his ability, preserve, protect, and defend the Constitution of the United States, and in violation of his constitutional duty to take care that the laws be faithfully executed, has failed without lawful cause or excuse to produce papers and things as directed by duly authorized subpoenas issued by the Committee on the Judiciary of the House of Representatives on April 11, 1974, May 15, 1974, May 30, 1974, and June 24, 1974, and willfully disobeyed such subpoenas. The subpoenaed papers and things were deemed necessary by the Committee in order to resolve by direct evidence fundamental, factual questions relating to Presidential direction, knowledge, or approval of actions demonstrated by other evidence to be substantial grounds for impeachment of the President. In refusing to produce these papers and things, Richard M. Nixon, substituting his judgment as to what materials were necessary for the inquiry, interposed the powers of the Presidency against the lawful subpoenas of the House of Representatives, thereby assuming to himself functions and judgments necessary to the exercise of the sole power of impeachment vested by the Constitution in the House of Representatives.

In all of this, Richard M. Nixon has acted in a manner contrary to his trust as President and subversive of constitutional government, to the great prejudice of the cause of law and justice, and to the manifest injury of the people of the United States.

Wherefore Richard M. Nixon, by such conduct, warrants impeachment and trial, and removal from office.

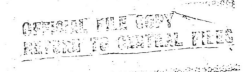

STATEMENT OF INFORMATION:

APPENDIX III

HEARINGS

BEFORE THE

COMMITTEE ON THE JUDICIARY

HOUSE OF REPRESENTATIVES

NINETY-THIRD CONGRESS

SECOND SESSION

PURSUANT TO

H. Res. 803

A RESOLUTION AUTHORIZING AND DIRECTING THE COMMITTEE
ON THE JUDICIARY TO INVESTIGATE WHETHER SUFFICIENT
GROUNDS EXIST FOR THE HOUSE OF REPRESENTATIVES TO
EXERCISE ITS CONSTITUTIONAL POWER TO IMPEACH

RICHARD M. NIXON

PRESIDENT OF THE UNITED STATES OF AMERICA

SUPPLEMENTARY DOCUMENTS:

White House Edited Transcripts (April 4, 1972,
March 22, 1973, June 23, 1972); John Ehrlichman
Handwritten Notes; Affidavit of Bruce A. Kehrli

MAY–JUNE 1974

(Unintelligible)

P   (Unintelligible)....they've got a magnificent place --

H   No, they don't. See, that was all hand-held camera

without lighting - lousy place. It's good in content,

it's terrible in film quality.

P   (Unintelligible) Rose, she ought to be in here.

H   No, well let her in if you want to, sure --

P   That's right. Got so goddamned much (scratching noises)

H   Goddamned.

P   I understand, I just thought (unintelligible).

If I do, I just buzz.

H   Yeah. Ah --

P   Good, that's a very good paper at least (unintelligible).

The one thing they haven't got in there is the thing we

mentioned with regard to the Armed Services.

H   I covered that with Ehrlichman who says that can be done

and he's moving. Not only Armed Services, but the whole

government.

P   GSA? All government?

H   All government procurement, yeah. And, I talked to John

about that and he thought that was a good idea. So, Henry

NOTE: *These transcripts of three Presidential conversations on June 23, 1972, were submitted to the Committee at the direction of the President by James D. St. Clair, Special Counsel to the President, on August 5, 1974.*

(39)

gets back at 3:45.

P   I told Haig today that I'd see Rogers at 4:30.

H   Oh, good, O. K.

P   Well, if he gets back at 3:45, he won't be here until

4:00 or 4:30.

H   It'll be a little after 4:00 (unintelligible) 5:00.

P   Well, I have to, I'm supposed to go to Camp David.

Rogers doesn't need a lot of time, does he?

H   No sir.

P   Just a picture?

H   That's all. He called me about it yesterday afternoon and

said I don't want to be in the meeting with Henry, I understand

that but there may be a couple of points Henry wants me to

be aware of.

P   Sure.

P   (Unintelligible) call him and tell him we'll call him as

soon as Henry gets here, between 4:30 and 5:00 (unintelligible)

Good.

H   O. K., that's fine.

H   Now, on the investigation, you know the Democratic

break-in thing, we're back in the problem area because

the FBI is not under control, because Gray doesn't exactly

know how to control it and they have - their investigation

is now leading into some productive areas - because they've

(40)

been able to trace the money - not through the money itself -

but through the bank sources - the banker. And, and it

goes in some directions we don't want it to go. Ah, also

there have been some things - like an informant came in off

the street to the FBI in Miami who was a photographer or has

a friend who is a photographer who developed some films

through this guy Barker and the films had pictures of

Democratic National Committee letterhead documents and

things. So it's things like that that are filtering in. Mitchell

came up with yesterday, and John Dean analyzed very care-

fully last night and concludes, concurs now with Mitchell's

recommendation that the only way to solve this, and we're

set up beautifully to do it, ah, in that and that -- the only

network that paid any attention to it last night was NBC -

they did a massive story on the Cuban thing.

P   That's right.

H   That the way to handle this now is for us to have Walters call

Pat Gray and just say, "Stay to hell out of this - this is ah,

business here we don't want you to go any further on it."

That's not an unusual development, and ah, that would take

care of it.

P   What about Pat Gray -- you mean Pat Gray doesn't want to?

(41)

H   Pat does want to. He doesn't know how to, and he doesn't

     have, he doesn't have any basis for doing it. Given this,

     he will then have the basis. He'll call Mark Felt in, and

     the two of them -- and Mark Felt wants to cooperate because

     he's ambitious --

P   Yeah.

H   He'll call him in and say, "We've got the signal from across

     the river to put the hold on this." And that will fit rather

     well because the FBI agents who are working the case, at this

     point, feel that's what it is.

P   This is CIA? They've traced the money? Who'd they trace it

     to?

H   Well they've traced it to a name, but they haven't gotten to

     the guy yet.

P   Would it be somebody here?

H   Ken Dahlberg.

P   Who the hell is Ken Dahlberg?

H   He gave $25,000 in Minnesota and, ah, the check went

     directly to this guy Barker.

P   It isn't from the Committee though, from Stans?

H   Yeah. It is. It's directly traceable and there's some more

     through some Texas people that went to the Mexican bank

(42)

5

which can also be traced to the Mexican bank - they'll get their names today.

--And (pause) ;

Well, I mean, there's no way -- I'm just thinking if they don't cooperate, what do they say? That they were approached by the Cubans. That's what Dahlberg has to say, the Texans too, that they --

Well, if they will. But then we're relying on more and more people all the time. That's the problem and they'll stop if we could take this other route.

All right.

And you seem to think the thing to do is get them to stop?

Right, fine.

They say the only way to do that is from White House instructions. And it's got to be to Helms and to - ah, what's his name.....? Walters.

Walters.

And the proposal would be that Ehrlichman and I call them in, and say, ah --

All right, fine. How do you call him in -- I mean you just -- well, we protected Helms from one hell of a lot of things. That's what Ehrlichman says.

(43)

P   Of course, this Hunt, that will uncover a lot of things.

You open that scab there's a hell of a lot of things and

we just feel that it would be very detrimental to have this

thing go any further. This involves these Cubans, Hunt,

and a lot of hanky-panky that we have nothing to do with

ourselves. Well what the hell, did Mitchell know about

this?

H   I think so. I don't think he knew the details, but I think he

knew.

P   He didn't know how it was going to be handled though - with

Dahlberg and the Texans and so forth? Well who was the

asshole that did? Is it Liddy? Is that the fellow? He must

be a little nuts!

H   He is.

P   I mean he just isn't well screwed on is he? Is that the problem?

H   No, but he was under pressure, apparently, to get more

information, and as he got more pressure, he pushed the

people harder to move harder --

P   Pressure from Mitchell?

H   Apparently.

P   Oh, Mitchell. Mitchell was at the point (unintelligible).

H   Yeah.

(44)

P   All right, fine, I understand it all. We won't second-guess Mitchell and the rest. Thank God it wasn't Colson.

H   The FBI interviewed Colson yesterday. They determined that would be a good thing to do. To have him take an interrogation, which he did, and that - the FBI guys working the case concluded that there were one or two possibilities - one, that this was a White House - they don't think that there is anything at the Election Committee - they think it was either a White House operation and they had some obscure reasons for it - non-political, or it was a - Cuban and the CIA. And after their interrogation of Colson yesterday, they concluded it was not the White House, but are now convinced it is a CIA thing, so the CIA turnoff would --

P   Well, not sure of their analysis, I'm not going to get that involved. I'm (unintelligible).

H   No, sir, we don't want you to.

P   You call them in.

H   Good deal.

P   Play it tough. That's the way they play it and that's the way we are going to play it.

H   O. K.

P   When I saw that news summary, I questioned whether it's a

P   bunch of crap, but I thought, er, well it's good to have them

off us awhile, because when they start bugging us, which they

have, our little boys will not know how to handle it. I hope

they will though.

H   You never know.

P   Good.

H   Mosbacher has resigned.

P   Oh yeah?

H   As we expected he would.

P   Yeah.

H   He's going back to private life (unintelligible).

Do you want to sign this or should I send it to Rose?

P   (scratching noise)

H   Do you want to release it?

P   O. K. Great. Good job, Bob.

H   Kissinger?

P   Huh? That's a joke.

H   Is it?

P   Whenever Mosbacher came for dinners, you see he'd have

to be out escorting the person in and when they came through

the receiving line, Henry was always with Mrs. Mosbacher

and she'd turn and they would say this is Mrs. Kissinger. He

(46)

P   (Inaudible) our cause --

H   Get more done for our cause by the opposition than by us.

P   Well, can you get it done?

H   I think so.

P   (unintelligible) moves (unintelligible) election (unintelligible)

H   They're all -- that's the whole thing.   The <u>Washington</u> <u>Post</u>
     said it in it's lead editorial today.   Another "McGovern's
     got to change his position." That that would be a good thing,
     that's constructive.   Ah, the white wash for change.

P   (unintelligible) urging him to do so - say that is perfectly
     all right?

H   Cause then they are saying -- on the other hand -- that he
     were not so smart. We have to admire the progress he's
     made on the basis of the position he's taken and maybe he's
     right and we're wrong.

P   (Inaudible) I just, ha ha

H   Sitting in Miami (unintelligible) our hand a little bit.   They
     eliminated their law prohibiting male (unintelligible) from
     wearing female clothes - now the boys can all put on their
     dresses - so the gay lib is going to turn out 6,000 (unintelligible).

P   (unintelligible)

H   I think

(55)

H   Well he said you probably didn't need it. He didn't think

    you should -- not at all. He said he felt fine doing it.

P   He did? The question, the point, is does he think everybody

    is going to understand the bussing?

H   That's right.

P   And, ah, well (unintelligible) says no.

H   Well, the fact is somewhere in between, I think, because I

    think that (unintelligible) is missing some --

P   Well, if the fact is somewhere in between, we better do it.

H   Yeah, I think Mitchell says, "Hell yes. Anything we can hit

    on at anytime we get the chance -- and we've got a reason for

    doing it -- do it."

P   When you get in -- when you get in (unintelligible) people,

    say, "Look the problem is that this will open the whole, the

    whole Bay of Pigs thing, and the President just feels that ah,

    without going into the details -- don't, don't lie to them to

    the extent to say there is no involvement, but just say this is

    a comedy of errors, without getting into it, the President

    believes that it is going to open the whole Bay of Pigs thing

    up again. And, ah, because these people are plugging for

    (unintelligible) and that they should call the FBI in and

    (unintelligible) don't go any further into this case period!

(54)

3816

EXHIBIT NO. 130

28 June 1972

MEMORANDUM FOR RECORD

On 26 June at about 10:00 a.m. I received a phone call from
Mr. John Dean at the White House. He said he wished to see me
about the matter that John Ehrlichman and Bob Haldeman had
discussed with me on the 23rd of June. I could check this out
with them if I wished. I agreed to call on him in his office in
Room 106 at the Executive Office Building at 1145 that morning.
Immediately after hanging up, I called Ehrlichman to find out if
this was alright and after some difficulty I reached him and he
said I could talk freely to Dean.

At 1145 I called at Dean's office and saw him alone. He said
that the investigation of the Watergate "bugging" case was extremely
awkward, there were lots of leads to important people and that the
FBI which was investigating the matter was working on three theories:

1. It was organized by the Republican National Committee.
2. It was organized by the CIA.
3. It was organized by some other party.

I said that I had discussed this with Director Helms and I was
quite sure that the Agency was not in any way involved and I knew
that the Director wished to distance himself and the Agency from the
matter. Dean then asked whether I was sure that the Agency was not
involved. [   ]
                                    I said that I was sure that none of
the suspects had been on the Agency payroll for the last two years.

Dean then said that some of the accused were getting scared and
"wobbling". I said that even so they could not implicate the Agency.
Dean then asked whether there was not some way that the Agency
could pay bail for them (they had been unable to raise bail). He
added that it was not just bail, that if these men went to prison,
could we (CIA) find some way to pay their salaries while they were
in jail out of covert action funds.

3817

I said that I must be quite clear. I was the Deputy Director and as such had only authority specifically delegated to me by the Director and was not in the chain of command but that the great strength of the Agency and its value to the President of the nation lay in the fact that it was apolitical and had never gotten itself involved in political disputes. Despite the fact that I had only been with the Agency a short time, I knew that the Director felt strongly about this.

I then said that big as the troubles might be with the Watergate Affair, if the Agency were to provide bail and pay salaries, this would become known sooner or later in the current "leaking" atmosphere of Washington and at that point the scandal would be ten times greater as such action could only be done upon direction at the "highest level" and that those who were not touched by the matter now would certainly be so.

Dean seemed at first taken aback and then very much impressed by this argument and said that it was certainly a very great risk that would have to be weighed. I repeated that the present affair would be small potatoes compared to what would happen if we did what he wanted and it leaked. He nodded gravely.

I said that, in addition, the Agency would be completely discredited with the public and the Congress and would lose all value to the President and the Administration. Again he nodded gravely.

He then asked if I could think of any way we (CIA) could help. I said I could not think of any but I would discuss the matter with the Director and would be in touch with him. However, I felt that I was fully cognizant of the Director's feelings in this matter. He thanked me and I left.

                            Vernon A. Walters
                         Lieutenant General. USA

2

WATERGATE SPECIAL PROSECUTION FORCE   DEPARTMENT OF JUSTICE

Memorandum

TO   : Leon Jaworski   DATE: August 9, 1974
         Special Prosecutor

FROM : Carl B. Feldbaum
         Peter M. Kreindler

SUBJECT: Factors to be Considered in Deciding Whether to
         Prosecute Richard M. Nixon for Obstruction of
         Justice
──

In our view there is clear evidence that Richard M. Nixon
participated in a conspiracy to obstruct justice by concealing
the identity of those responsible for the Watergate break-in
and other criminal offenses. There is a presumption (which in
the past we have operated upon) that Richard M. Nixon, like
every citizen, is subject to the rule of law. Accordingly,
one begins with the premise that if there is sufficient evidence, Mr. Nixon should be indicted and prosecuted. The
question then becomes whether the presumption for proceeding
is outweighed by the factors mandating against indictment and
prosecution.

The factors which mandate against indictment and prosecution are:

   1. His resignation has been sufficient punishment.

   2. He has been subject to an impeachment inquiry
       with resulting articles of impeachment which
       the House Judiciary Committee unanimously
       endorsed as to Article I (the Watergate
       cover-up).

   3. Prosecution might aggravate political
       divisions in the country.

   4. As a political matter, the times call for
       conciliation rather than recrimination.

   5. There would be considerable difficulty in
       achieving a fair trial because of massive
       pre-trial publicity.

The factors which mandate in favor of indictment and prosecution are:

1. The principle of equal justice under law requires that every person, no matter what his past position or office, answer to the criminal justice system for his past offenses. This is a particularly weighty factor if Mr. Nixon's aides and associates, who acted upon his orders and what they conceived to be his interests, are to be prosecuted for the same offenses.

2. The country will be further divided by Mr. Nixon unless there is a final disposition of charges of criminality outstanding against him so as to forestall the belief that he was driven from his office by erosion of his political base. This final disposition may be necessary to preserve the integrity of the criminal justice system and the legislative process, which together marshalled the substantial evidence of Mr. Nixon's guilt.

3. Article I, Section 3, clause 7 of the Constitution provides that a person removed from office by impeachment and conviction "shall nevertheless be liable and subject to Indictment, Trial, Judgment, and Punishment, according to Law." The Framers contemplated that a person removed from office because of abuse of his public trust still would have to answer to the criminal justice system for criminal offenses.

4. It cannot be sufficient retribution for criminal offenses merely to surrender the public office and trust which has been demonstrably abused. A person should not be permitted to trade in the abused office in return for immunity.

5. The modern nature of the Presidency necessitates massive public exposure of the President's actions through the media. A bar to prosecution on the grounds of such publicity effectively would immunize all future Presidents for their actions, however criminal. Moreover, the courts may be the appropriate forum to resolve questions of pre-trial publicity in the context of an adversary proceeding.

- 3 -

    6. There is a definite long-term interest in
       assuring full disclosure of public corruption.

The factors which mandate in favor of delaying this decision
are:

    1. Neither this office, Congress, nor the public has
       had sufficient time to consider the cataclysmic _ended_
       events which began only this Monday and ~~~~~ on
       the President's resignation today.

    2. This office will be reviewing important evidence
       which will have to be analyzed and weighed. This
       evidence may bear heavily on this decision.

    3. Since both the factors which weigh in favor of
       and against the indictment and prosecution of Mr.
       Nixon implicate political considerations in the
       highest sense, it will be important in weighing
       these factors to determine whether the Congress
       and public coalesce behind a predominant view.
       Moreover, it will be important to consider how
       the public will view the decision in hindsight,
       after all the evidence is available.

    4. There has been considerable concern about the
       interaction with and the affect of this decision
       on the Watergate trial. It now appears that
       there will be at least some delay in the trial,
       which will give this office more time to con-
       sider these interrelationships. In addition,
       there may be guilty pleas which could affect
       the decision of whether to indict and prosecute
       Mr. Nixon.

Finally, in weighing these factors, one should not ignore
the possibility of a disposition of Mr. Nixon's offenses by a
plea.

cc: Mr. Vorenberg
     Mr. Lacovara

The Washington Post

Carrie Johnson

Finding That 'Point of Pure Justice'

SPOKANE—"It's been very traumatic. People have cried and been down in the dumps. But now it's over and maybe we can talk about something else."

That's how Spokane County's Republican chairman, Homer F. Cunningham, sums up the mood in this city of 170,000 in the hills of eastern Washington. This has been Nixon country for a long, long time. But when President Nixon resigned and his portrait at the U.S. pavilion at Expo '74 was taken down, the first general reaction here as elsewhere was relief.

In more than two dozen conversations with civic leaders and ordinary voters here, another theme emerges as well. For many, Mr. Nixon's downfall has become a matter of law, not politics. That attitude, if widespread, could have tremendous bearing on long-term public opinion about whether and how the former President should be called to account.

According to persons active in both parties here, most Spokanites discounted Watergate, until very recently, as another partisan fracas, a dispute among politicians who all have dirty hands. The local mood began to change, two Democrats believed, when the House Judiciary Committee's televised sessions began. Then, one said, "people could see this wasn't just politics but a serious problem."

Especially for Republicans, the June 23 transcripts were decisive. Mr. Nixon's offenses were suddenly defined, by his own words, as a clear, unavoidable question of crime. "Crime" seems to have an elementary meaning here. It does not mean debatable abuses of special presidential powers. It does not mean contempt of Congress, since Congress is held in rather low repute. "Crime" means the obvious: lying when one had pledged to tell the truth, concealing evidence, and obstruction of justice—a phrase which has become a layman's term.

And crime means courts, verdicts and punishment. Based on a small, unscientific sampling, opinion here is fragmented on whether Mr. Nixon

should be prosecuted. Some, including most Republicians contacted, thought that the public verdict had been rendered and that the disgrace of resignation was punishment enough. "What more can you do to the guy?" one GOP leader asked.

Richard J. Schroeder, an attorney and county Democratic chairman, took a contrasting view. Mr. Nixon's resignation was not conclusive, Schroeder felt. "From what I understand, he and John Dean did about the same things in obstructing justice. He should be brought before the courts and made to answer like everyone else."

As Schroeder himself acknowledged, this seemed to be a minority view. For a number of people, however, the question was a difficult and troubling one.

"About 20 of us were talking about it over a campfire in northern Idaho last night," said A. J. Pardini, a GOP state

---

The writer is a member of the editorial page staff.

---

legislator. "We couldn't work it out. Most of us wanted no further prosecution of Nixon—except for the implications for the other people on trial."

Pardini thought that younger people, regardless of their political philosophy were more skeptical about "the system" and more inclined to favor prosecution. "Those over about 35 are more compassionate," he suggested.

For Pardini himself, however, compassion seemed to collide with a basic sense of fairness. In separate conversations, three women expressed a similar ambivalence in different terms. One, a professor's wife who said she "leaned Republican," stated, "I think he probably should be prosecuted." Then, after a pause, she added, "But I don't want to see it."

The second, a department-store clerk, commented, "Worse people than he have gotten off. But I don't really know what's fair."

The third, a banker's wife, remarked, "I do feel sorry for the man.

But I also feel sorry for everyone else connected with this garbage who is serving time or has already gotten out of jail. I wish someone could find a way to handle this outside of politics—to get it down to the point of pure justice."

That seemed to be a common wish: a desire to find some unmistakable "point of pure justice" on which to conclude, in an obviously non-political way, the gravest political scandal in the nation's history.

No clear definition of "pure justice" emerged from these conversations in one moderate-to-conservative community. What did emerge was the wisdom of Special Pro-prosecutor Leon Jaworski's decision to do nothing precipitious, and the even greater wisdom of the apparent decisions by Congress and President Ford, the "politicans," to do nothing about immunity or prosecution at all.

It may be that the question is too difficult, that there is no course which avoids arousing new hostility—if only among that considerable segment of the populace which simply doesn't want to think about the subject any more.

It may be, on the other hand, that a generally acceptable solution wll develop through legal processes, through events related to the forthcoming trial of Mr. Nixon's aides and his own conduct as a subpoenaed witness.

To some people here, at least, the law should be the final standard and arbiter. That came through most clearly in the comments of one Republican voter, the wife of a retired city clerk, who talked about the scandal while mowing her small front lawn, on the morning Mr. Nixon left office.

"I feel very sorry for the family," she said. "But he didn't apologize and we still don't know whether he's guilty of anything or not. I think there's a lot that still needs to be brought out in the open."

She had been speaking slowly. But when asked where the matter ought to be aired, she answered quickly, almost reflexively: "Why, in the courts!"

WATERGATE SPECIAL PROSECUTION FORCE

Memorandum

DEPARTMENT OF JUSTICE

TO : Leon Jaworski
     Special Prosecutor

DATE: September 5, 1974

FROM : Philip A. Lacovara
       Counsel to the Special
          Prosecutor

SUBJECT: Possible Pardon of Richard Nixon

       I have earlier written to you recommending that you con-
tact the White House to ascertain whether President Ford has
decided to exercise executive clemency in favor of former
President Nixon and if so to urge that this be done immediately,
obviating the prosecutorial determination whether or not to
charge Mr. Nixon. I also urge, however, that you affirmatively
recommend that any pardon which President Ford may be inclined
to issue be a conditional one. As you know, and as the recent
litigation over former President Nixon's extension of clemency
to James Hoffa underscored, a President's flexibility in granting pardons or commutation is considerable. Conditional pardons are not uncommon and in the present circumstances legiti-
mate law enforcement interests and the elementary notions of
fairness seem to me to require that at least two conditions be
attached to any pardon to Mr. Nixon:

       1. The first condition should be a full and formal
acknowledgement by Mr. Nixon of his complicity in the Watergate cover-up. Although the mere acceptance of a pardon tech-
nically constitutes an acknowledgement of criminal complicity
without more, I believe more is required here. Mr. Nixon
(like former Vice President Agnew who was permitted to plead
nolo contendere to one criminal charge) has continued to main-
tain his complete innocence of any wrongdoing. Today's news-
papers carried statements by Mr. Nixon's son-in-law, David
Eisenhower, indicating that the former President intends to
remain active in American political life and perhaps to attempt
to return to public office -- courses that would certainly have
been foreclosed to him if the impeachment process had been
allowed to run its course. We now know on the basis of the
tapes that are becoming available to us pursuant to the Supreme
Court's decision in United States v. Nixon that Mr. Nixon's
involvement in the Watergate cover-up was far more extensive
and aggressive than even John Dean knew or we could speculate.

In addition to the disclosures on the June 23, 1972 tape which
show that the former President endorsed the effort to fob off
the Watergate investigation at the outset by misusing federal
agencies, the January 8, 1973 conversation with Charles Colson
shows that the former President at that time was personally
aware of and approved the payment of "hush money" and was
actively working with Mr. Colson to promise a pardon to defend-
ant Howard Hunt and early parole to the other defendants in
order to buy their silence. For reasons of trial tactics,
such tapes may not actually be used at the Watergate trial. I
believe it would be a monstrous act to leave the historical
record as cloudy as it is now, even on the basis of the Judiciary
Committee's inquiry, when we have in our possession evidence of
the most persistent and intensive public corruption imaginable.
I would not insist on public self-flagellation by Mr. Nixon but
I cannot see any just alternative to the most strenuous recommendation from this office that any pardon to Mr. Nixon by con-
ditioned on his formal public acknowledgement of complicity in
the Watergate conspiracy.

    2. The additional condition that I believe you should
press vigorously involves continued access to the White House
files accumulated during the Nixon Presidency. Even accepting
the highly questionable conclusion of the Department of Justice
that these masses of tapes and documents are the private
property of Mr. Nixon, we know that they contain substantial
quantities of evidence bearing on investigations actively underway within the jurisdiction of this Office. I am not recom-
mending that we insist on "rummaging" through those files on an
exploratory frolic. Rather, I believe you should urge the
importance of a formal condition that guarantees us access,
without the need for litigation, to those tapes and files
which we can identify with reasonable specificity as bearing
on particular investigations already underway. Indeed, we have
been lodging strong objections with the White House and the
Department of Justice to any course that would complicate our
ability to secure access to evidence that is pertinent to
investigations that are assigned to us. It seems only prudent
to build in a guarantee of cooperation, to this limited extent,
in connection with any pardon that may be extended to Mr. Nixon
on grounds unrelated to his own personal innocence or to the
innocence of his aides who are currently under indictment or
investigation.

    Although it has a touch of irony, in light of the condition
that Mr. Nixon attached to the Hoffa commutation (the validity

- 2 -

of which was recently upheld by the district court here), you might also point out to White House counsel the possibility of conditioning a pardon on Mr. Nixon's agreement not to seek public office again. Although such a term is one that is beyond the ambit of our official interest and might be politically difficult for the new President, it would bear on matters within our jurisdiction: if a pardon is extended to Mr. Nixon but not to those people who acted on his behalf and have either "paid the price" for their offenses or are being put to trial for them, then it would seem important to see to it that, to the extent possible, the disparity of treatment is minimized. A condition of a pardon that foreclosed efforts to recapture public office would tend to equalize the results, even though Mr. Nixon would be spared the ignominy and hardship of prosecution and possible confinement and would simply be limited to receiving his lifetime pension and emoluments and engaging in any other private activities that remain open to him.

cc: Mr. Ruth
    Mr. Kreindler

- 3 -

Ladies and gentlemen, I have come to a decision which I felt I should tell you, and all my fellow citizens, as soon as I was certain in my own mind and conscience that it is the right thing to do.

I have learned already in this office that only the difficult decisions come to this desk. I ~~frankly~~ must admit that many of them do not look at all the same as the hypothetical questions that I have answered freely and perhaps too fast on previous occasions. ~~It is my regular custom~~ My customary policy is to try and get all the facts and to consider the opinions of my countrymen and to take counsel with my most valued friends. But these ~~persons~~ seldom agree, and in the end the decision is mine.

~~And to delay,~~ To procrastinate, to agonize, to wait for a more favorable turn of events that may never come, or more compelling external pressures that may as well be wrong as right, is/a decision of sorts and a itself weak and ~~cowardly,xsomexasxwell~~ potentially dangerous ~~one~~ course for a President ~~xxcourse~~ to follow.

I have promised to uphold the Constitution, to ℗ do what is right as God gives me to see the right, and to do the very best I can for America. I have asked your help and your prayers, not only when I became President, but many times since.

The Constitution is the supreme law of our land and it governs our actions as citizens. Only the laws of God, which govern our consciences, are superior to it. As we are a Nation under God, so I am sworn to uphold our laws with the help of God. And I have sought such guidance and searched my own conscience with special diligence to determine the right thing for me to do with respect to my predecessor in this place, Richard Nixon, and his ~~wonderful~~ loyal wife and family.

Theirs is an American tragedy in which we all have
played a part. It can go on and on +m or someone must write
"the end" to it.

I have concluded that only I can do that. And if I
can, I must.

There are no historic or legal precedents to which
I can turn in this matter, none that precisely fit the
circumstances of a private citizen who has resigned the
Presidency of the United States. But it is common knowledge that serious allegations and accusations hang like
a xxxxxx sword over our Former President's head as he tries
to reshape his life, a great part of which was spent in the
                                                    its
service of this country and by the mandate of the people.

After years of bitter controversy and divisive national
debate, I have been advised and am compelled to conclude that
                      more
many months and perhaps/years will have to pass before Richard
Nixon could hope to obtain a fair trial by jury in any jurisdiction of the United States under governing decisions of the
Supreme Court.

I deeply believe in equal justice for all Americans,
whatever their station or former station. The law, whether
human or Divine, is no respecter of persons but the law is
a respecter of reality. The facts as I see them are that a
former President of the United States, instead of enjoying
equal treatment with any other citizen accused of violating
the law, would be cruelly and excessively penalized either in

preserving the
~~establishing his~~ presumption of *his* innocence or in obtaining a

speedy determination of his guilt in order to repay a legal

debt to society.

During this long period of delay and potential litigation,

ugly passions would again be aroused, our people would again

be polarized in their opinions, and the credibility of our free

institutions of government would again be challenged at home and

abroad. In the end, the courts might well hold that Richard

verdict of history
Nixon had been denied due process and the ~~result~~ would be even

arising out of
more inconclusive with respect to those charges ~~against him during~~

~~during~~ the period of
~~which I am now aware pertaining to~~ his Presidency of which I

am presently aware.

But it is not the ultimate fate of Richard Nixon that most

surely it
concerns me -- though ~~it must~~ deeply trouble*s* every decent and

Rather my concern is
compassionate person -- ~~but~~ the immediate future of this great

depend upon
country. In this I dare not ~~subordinate it must~~ my personal ~~feel~~

sympathy   longtime
~~know~~ as a/friend of the Former President ~~for 25 years~~ nor my

professional judgment as a lawyer. And I do not.

As President, my primary concern must always be the greatest

good of all the people of the United States, whose servant I am.

As a man, my first consideration ~~will always be~~ to be true

to my own convictions and my own conscience.

My conscience tells me clearly and certainly that I cannot

prolong the bad dreams that continue to reopen a chapter that

is closed. My conscience tells me that only I, as president,

have the Constitutional power to firmly shut and seal this book.

My conscience says it is my duty, not merely to proclaim domestic

tranquillity, but to use every means I have to ensure it.

4

~~Finally,~~ I do believe that the buck stops here and that I cannot rely upon public opinion polls to tell me what is right. I do believe that right makes might, and that if I am wrong ~~all the legions of~~ ^{ten} angels swearing I was right would make no difference. I do believe with all my heart and ~~xxxixx~~ mind and spirit that I,/as President ^{not} ~~and~~ ^{but} as a humble servant of God, will receive justice without mercy if I fail to show mercy.

~~Ixkx~~ Finally, I feel that Richard Nixon and his loved ones have suffered enough, and will continue t_o suffer no matter what ~~xixxxxxxx~~ ^{I do, ~~xxxxxx~~ no matter what} we as a great and good Nation can d_o together to make his ~~dream~~ ^{goal} of peace ~~xxxxxxxx~~ ~~xxxxxxx~~ come true.

"Now, therefore, I, Gerald R. Ford

3

NOW, THEREFORE, I, Gerald R. Ford, President of the

United States, pursuant to the pardon power conferred upon me by

Article II, Section 2, of the Constitution, have granted and by these

presents do grant a full, free, and absolute pardon unto Richard Nixon

for all offenses against the United States which he, Richard Nixon, has

committed or may have committed or taken part in during the period

from January 20, 1969 through August 9, 1974.

IN WITNESS WHEREOF, I have hereunto set my hand this

8th day of September in the year of our Lord Nineteen Hundred

Seventy-Four, and of the Independence of the United States of

America the 199th.

_____

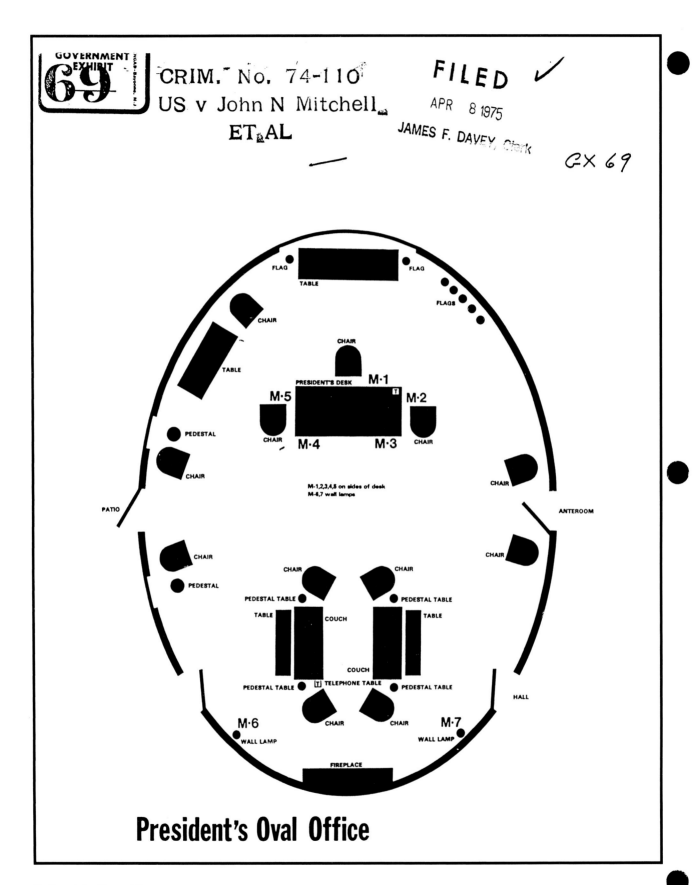

President's Oval Office

Suggestions for Further Reading

The literature about Watergate is voluminous. Myron Smith's bibliography, for example, lists over 2,500 entries for books and articles published through 1982. This select list emphasizes participants' accounts.

Bernstein, Carl, and Bob Woodward. *All the President's Men.* New York: Simon and Schuster, 1974.

Congressional Quarterly. *Watergate: Chronology of a Crisis.* Washington, DC: Congressional Quarterly, 1973.

Dean, John W. *Blind Ambition: The White House Years.* New York: Simon and Schuster, 1982.

Ehrlichman, John. *Witness to Power: The Nixon Years.* New York: Simon and Schuster, 1982.

Ervin, Samuel James. *The Whole Truth: The Watergate Conspiracy.* New York: Random House, 1980.

Haldeman, H. R. *The Ends of Power.* New York: Times Books, 1978.

Jaworski, Leon. *The Right and the Power: The Prosecution of Watergate.* New York: Reader's Digest Press, 1976.

Nixon, Richard M. *RN: The Memoirs of Richard Nixon.* New York: Grosset and Dunlap, 1978.

————. *In the Arena: A Memoir of Victory, Defeat, and Renewal.* New York: Simon and Schuster, 1990.

The Presidential Transcripts. New York: Delacorte, 1974. *(Washington Post)*

Sirica, John. *To Set the Record Straight: The Break-in, the Tapes, the Conspirators, the Pardon.* New York: Norton, 1979.

Smith, Myron J. *Watergate: An Annotated Bibliography of Sources in English, 1972–1982.* Metuchen, NJ: Scarecrow, 1983.

United States v. Nixon, 418 U.S. 683.

The White House Transcripts. New York: Viking, 1974. *(New York Times)*

Woodward, Bob, and Carl Bernstein, *The Final Days.* New York: Simon and Schuster, 1976.

About Using the National Archives

A Word to Students and Educators

The National Archives and Records Administration (NARA) is the federal agency responsible for preserving and making available to the public the permanently valuable records of the federal government. These materials provide evidence of the activities of the government from 1774 to the present in the form of written and printed documents, maps and posters, sound recordings, photographs, films, computer tapes, and other information media. These rich archival sources are useful to everyone: to federal officials seeking information about past activities of their agencies; to citizens needing data for use in legal matters; to lawyers, historians, social scientists and public policy planners, engineers, medical researchers, novelists and playwrights, journalists researching stories, and people tracing their ancestry or satisfying their curiosity about particular historical events. In particular, these records are useful to you in pursuing your own research, whether professional or personal.

The organization and description of records in an archives differs from that of books in a library in three significant ways. First, the records are maintained under the name of the agency or bureau that created them rather than under a system of classification such as would be found in a library using the Dewey decimal system or Library of Congress classifications, for example. Instead, each discrete body of records is assigned a record group number; thus the records of the Department of State are arbitrarily designated Record Group 59, and the records of the Bureau of Indian Affairs are arbitrarily designated Record Group 75. There are more than 400 record groups in the National Archives representing the records of as many bureaus, agencies, and departments of the federal government.

Second, records are maintained in the same order as they were maintained in the agency that created them, allowing the researcher to examine how the agency's understanding of its mission was reflected in its organization. The records of two agencies, bureaus, or departments are never intermixed, however similar their functions. Thus the records of the National Park Service (RG 79) and those of the Forest Service (RG 95) are maintained separately, even though they both have responsibility for public lands.

Finally, the National Archives does not, for the most part, use card catalogs or other library tools to describe its holdings. Rather, it provides narrative descriptions of record groups called inventories or preliminary inventories and also publishes a *Guide to the National Archives of the United States*, which provides brief descriptions of each record group. This form of description is now typical of most larger archives and manuscript collections, which have long since abandoned costly item-by-item description in favor of a method that provides the researcher an overview of an entire collection whose separate items have meaning only in the context of those items around them.

NARA is a public institution whose records and research facilities nationwide are open to anyone 16 years of age and older who will use the records according to the simple rules laid out for their protection. These facilities are found in the Washington, DC, area, in the 8 Presidential libraries across the country and the Nixon Presidential Materials Staff in Alexandria, VA, and in the 12 regional archives ranging from Boston to Anchorage. Whether you are pursuing broad historical questions or are interested in the history of your family, admittance to the research room at each of these locations requires only that you fill out a simple form stating your name, address, and research interest. A staff member issues an identification card, which is good for 2 years.

If you come to the National Archives or its outlying research facilities, you will be offered an initial interview with a reference archivist. You will also be able to talk with archivists who work directly with the records you want. The best preparation for using the valuable information that these interviews provide is to have a clear definition of your questions and to have read as much as possible in the secandary sources before you arrive. A sound knowledge of the facts of your topic and its historical context is your best preparation for research in primary sources. Among the essential information you must develop before you arrive is the link between your topic and the function of the federal government. You will find information in the National Archives about litigation at the federal level, for example, but not at the state level. You will find information about population numbers and distribution because the federal government conducts a diennial census. You will find information about the Constitutional Convention, which was a national function, but not about the meetings of the Virginia House of Burgesses, which was both a colonial and prefederal institution. You will find vital statistics for Native American reservations and military posts because these are maintained by the federal government, but not for cities, which are not federal entities.

The best printed source of information about the holdings of the National Archives is the *Guide to the National Archives of the United States* (GPO, 1988), available in university libraries, other research institutions, and some public libraries. The *Guide* describes briefly each record group, gives the background and history of each agency represented by those records, and provides useful information about access to them. To accommodate users outside of Washington, DC, the regional archives hold microfilm copies of much that is found in Washington. In addition, the regional archives contain records created by field offices of the federal government, including district and appellate court records. These records are particularly useful for local and regional history studies and in linking local with national historic events.

If you are interested in the educational and cultural programs of the National Archives, the Education Branch of the Office of Public Programs provides these learning packages, a newsletter for 2-year college instructors, teacher workshops attended by instructors from precollegiate and collegiate levels, a theater program, and courses in using the Archives for genealogical and general

research. The Office of Public Programs also mounts exhibits of records; publishes exhibition catalogs, reproductions of records, and guides to holdings; and develops special events and tours. For information about these programs, write to Office of Public Programs, NARA, Washington, DC 20408.

The Presidential Libraries:

Herbert Hoover Library
P.O. Box 488
West Branch, IA 52358

Franklin D. Roosevelt Library
511 Albany Post Road
Hyde Park, NY 12538

Harry S. Truman Library
Independence, MO 64050

Dwight D. Eisenhower Library
Abilene, KS 67410

John F. Kennedy Library
Columbia Point
Boston, MA 02125

Lyndon Baines Johnson Library
2313 Red River Street
Austin, TX 78705

Gerald R. Ford Library
1000 Beal Avenue
Ann Arbor, MI 48109

Jimmy Carter Library
One Copenhill Avenue
Atlanta, GA 30307

Nixon Presidential Materials Staff
845 South Pickett Street
Alexandria, VA 22304

Ronald Reagan Library
40 Presidential Drive
Simi Valley, CA 93065

National Archives Regional Archives:

National Archives—New England Region
380 Trapelo Road
Waltham, MA 02154

National Archives—Northeast Region
Bldg. 22, Military Ocean Terminal
Bayonne, NJ 07002

National Archives—Mid Atlantic Region
Ninth & Market Streets
Philadelphia, PA 19107

National Archives—Southeast Region
1557 St. Joseph Avenue
East Point, GA 30344

National Archives—Great Lakes Region
7358 South Pulaski Road
Chicago, IL 60629

National Archives—Central Plains Region
2312 East Bannister Road
Kansas City, MO 64131

National Archives—Southwest Region
501 West Felix Street
Fort Worth, TX 76115

National Archives—Rocky Mountain Region
Bldg. 48, Denver Federal Center
Denver, CO 80225

National Archives—Pacific Sierra Region
1000 Commodore Drive
San Bruno, CA 94066

National Archives—Pacific Southwest Region
24000 Avila Road
Laguna Niguel, CA 92677

National Archives—Pacific Northwest Region
6125 Sand Point Way
Seattle, WA 98115

National Archives—Alaska Region
654 West Third Avenue
Anchorage, AK 99501